YOUNG PROFILES

Kelly Clarkson

Jill C. Wheeler
ABDO Publishing Company

visit us at
www.abdopub.com

Published by ABDO Publishing Company, 4940 Viking Drive, Edina, Minnesota 55435.
Copyright © 2003 by Abdo Consulting Group, Inc. International copyrights reserved in
all countries. No part of this book may be reproduced in any form without written
permission from the publisher.

Printed in the United States.

Cover Photo: Image Direct
Interior Photos: AP/Wide World pp. 5, 9, 17, 20, 23, 31; Corbis p. 21; Image Direct pp. 7,
    11, 13, 14, 15, 18, 19, 22, 24, 25, 27, 29

Editors: Kate A. Conley, Stephanie Hedlund, Jennifer R. Krueger
Art Direction: Neil Klinepier

Library of Congress Cataloging-in-Publication Data

Wheeler, Jill C., 1964-
    Kelly Clarkson / Jill C. Wheeler.
      p. cm. -- (Young profiles)
    Summary: A biography of the twenty-year-old singer from Burleson, Texas, who
achieved overnight fame and a million dollar recording contract after winning the talent
contest on the television show, "American Idol."
    Includes bibliographical references and index.
    ISBN 1-57765-994-5
    1. Clarkson, Kelly, 1982---Juvenile literature. 2. Singers--United
States--Biography--Juvenile literature. [1. Clarkson, Kelly, 1982- 2. Singers.] I. Title.
II. Television Series.

ML3930.C523 W4 2003
782.42164'092--dc21
[B]
                                                                              2002038559

Contents

America's Idol

It reads like a fairy tale. A small-town girl becomes an overnight superstar. For Kelly Clarkson, it's more than a fairy tale. It's her life.

Kelly captured the hearts and votes of many Americans in the summer of 2002. That's when she appeared on a television show called *American* **Idol**. It was a national talent competition.

More people watched *American Idol* than any other show that summer. In fact, more than 20 million people tuned in for the final **episode**. Millions of people soon knew Kelly's name, face, and amazing voice.

Opposite page: Kelly Clarkson sings through tears after being named the American Idol.

Profile of an American Idol

Name: Kelly Brianne Clarkson
Birth Date: April 24, 1982
Place of Birth: Burleson, Texas
Height: Five feet, four inches
Parents: Jeanne and Jimmy (stepfather) Taylor and Steve Clarkson
Siblings: Jason and Alyssa
Nickname: Kellbell
Favorite Album: *Jagged Little Pill* by Alanis Morissette
Favorite Pop Artists: Mariah Carey, Celine Dion, Aretha Franklin, Whitney Houston
Favorite Singer: Reba McEntire
Favorite Food: Frozen Ding Dongs
Favorite Expression: "Cool beans"

Kelly Clarkson

Texas Roots

Kelly Clarkson was born in Burleson, Texas, on April 24, 1982. Her parents, Jeanne and Steve Clarkson, divorced when Kelly was six. Kelly's father later moved to California. But Kelly remained in Texas with her mother. Kelly's mother later married a **contractor** named Jimmy Taylor.

Kelly showed talent for singing and acting at an early age. Her family remembers her performing in the living room. Her productions included *Beauty and the Beast* and *The Little Mermaid*.

Kelly's mother recalls that the toughest part about raising Kelly was waking her in the morning. "When they say she sometimes went [to school] in her pajamas, they mean it," said Kelly's mother. "The alarm clock would be blasting right beside her head, and she didn't hear a thing. The house could have fallen apart and she'd still be sleeping."

Kelly Clarkson

A Big Voice

In the seventh grade, a teacher **recruited** Kelly for the school choir. Kelly's powerful voice stood out immediately. At home, Kelly practiced making her own recordings. She would put a **karaoke** machine in her closet. Then, she'd hang a sign on the door that read "Kelly's Recording Studio."

Kelly continued to sing in the choir at Burleson High School. Several times, the school's choir took trips overseas. Kelly didn't have enough money to go. But friends and teachers donated the funds she needed for the trips.

Kelly also earned important roles in her high school's musicals *Seven Brides for Seven Brothers* and *Brigadoon*. She found time to play volleyball, too. But Kelly didn't date much in high school. Instead, she concentrated on her music.

Opposite page: Kelly sings during "American Idol in Vegas."

She Writes, Too!

Not only did Kelly enjoy singing songs, she also liked writing them. After school, she often came home and wrote. She composed songs and poems about events in her life.

One of her favorite songs is called "Baby Blue Eyes." The song is about her high school crush. Kelly had a crush on one of her coworkers at Hollywood Theaters in Burleson. Unfortunately, her coworker already had a girlfriend.

Kelly quickly replaced her dreams of dating with career goals. People close to Kelly believed she had what it would take to succeed. "She always stressed that her career came first," said a friend. "She always believed that one day she'd be famous. She has a drive like I've never seen before."

Opposite page: Kelly Clarkson performs on American Idol.

Moving On

Kelly graduated from Burleson High School in 2000. She wanted to begin her music career right away. So she recorded a **demo** tape of her own songs. Then she sent copies of it to people in the music industry.

Kelly Clarkson

Kelly also worked at several different jobs. She sang in shows at an amusement park. She also worked as a waitress and drugstore clerk.

In 2002, one of Kelly's friends moved to Los Angeles, California. Kelly joined her and began to make contacts. She landed a tiny role on an **episode** of *Sabrina, the Teenage Witch*. She also began working with well-known songwriter Gerry Goffin.

Kelly's life seemed to be moving in the right direction. Then everything started to fall apart. Kelly's apartment building burned down, and her car was towed. Suddenly, she had nowhere to go.

Kelly spent several days in a homeless shelter. Finally, she decided to return to Texas. "She was discouraged at that point," her mother said. "She would always say to me, 'I have to sing; I don't know what else to do.'"

Kelly attends Jaguar's Tribute to Style in September 2002.

Idol Audition

Shortly after Kelly returned to Texas, her best friend, Jessica Huggins, signed her up for an upcoming **audition**. It was for a new television show called *American* **Idol**.

The concept for *American Idol* began in the United Kingdom. There, it was called *Pop Idol*. Now, the concept had come to the United States.

Kelly was one of 10,000 people to audition for *American Idol*. Everyone auditioning was between the ages of 16 and 24. Seven cities around the United States hosted auditions. Kelly was one of about 1,000 people who tried out in Dallas, Texas.

Kelly was terrified of sleeping through her alarm and missing the audition. So she stayed awake all night. Jessica recalled that at four A.M., Kelly threw rocks at her window to wake her.

Kelly sings a duet with Will Young, winner of Pop Idol,
during the final episode of American Idol.

Back to California

Kelly had to sing one **a cappella** song for the **audition**. Afterward, the judges called her back to sing two more songs. The judges selected Kelly as one of only 11 finalists from Dallas. Just months after leaving California, she was going back to compete in *American **Idol***.

In California, Kelly joined 120 singers from around the nation. On the first day, judges narrowed that list down to 65 singers. Then, they cut it to just 45 on the second day. After three days, only 30 contestants remained.

Kelly
Clarkson

The young singers listened eagerly as one of the judges, Simon Cowell, told them what lay ahead. He said, "One of you here is going to be the most famous person in America: The American Idol."

Kelly sings with her American Idol *costars.*

R-E-S-P-E-C-T

Kelly and the other contestants soon learned that *American* **Idol**'s first round would last three weeks. The contestants would compete against each other. Each week a different group of 10 contestants would sing. At the end of each song, the judges would **critique** the performance.

American Idol judges (from left to right): Simon Cowell, Paula Abdul, and Randy Jackson

At the end of the show, viewers would call in their votes. Voting results would be announced on the following **episode**. Only 10 contestants would move on after the first round.

Now the hard work began. The contestants received advice on how

to dress and perform.
They also began working
with a **vocal** coach. This
was a new experience for
Kelly. "I've never had
formal voice lessons or
anything," she said. "For
the most part I pretty
much do everything on
my own. . . . I know my
voice and what I can do.
I want to go with what
my gut says."

Kelly performs during the final episode of competition on September 3, 2002.

Kelly's turn to perform came during the show's second week. She sang "Respect" by Aretha Franklin, one of her favorite artists. Kelly's performance impressed the judges and the **audience**. Nearly 7 million viewers voted. Kelly received enough votes to move on. She returned to Burleson for a brief visit in late June. Her hometown gave her a star's welcome.

A Star in Training

For the next few weeks, Kelly and nine other finalists worked in Los Angeles and lived in a Hollywood mansion. Each week, they performed on the television show. And each week, more finalists were eliminated.

Kelly had never sung so much before. Often, she only slept three or four hours a night. Soon, her voice became hoarse. So she sucked on throat **lozenges** and gulped olive oil to keep her voice in shape.

Kelly's sleek style

Along the way, she worked with hair, makeup, and **wardrobe** stylists. Kelly chose a different wardrobe than many of the other female contestants. She chose not to wear revealing outfits. Instead, she developed a sleek, **sophisticated** look.

In August, Kelly returned to Texas. She visited her old high school and talked with reporters about how the show had affected her. "I just try to be as real as I can be," she said, "the kind of person who doesn't really care if she is caught without makeup."

Kelly Clarkson visits her old high school in Burleson, Texas.

An Idol Is Crowned

American **Idol**'s final competition occurred on Tuesday, September 3, 2002. Kelly Clarkson and Justin Guarini were the final two contestants. Celebrities and fans alike packed Hollywood's Kodak Theatre to watch the show.

At home, 23 million people tuned in to see Kelly compete against Justin. Kelly and Justin each sang three songs. Kelly's performance of "Respect" brought **audience** members to their feet.

Kelly Clarkson and Justin Guarini hug after learning Kelly is the American Idol.

For two hours following the show, people called in their votes. The results would be announced the next day, on *American **Idol**'s* final **episode**.

More than 500 Burleson residents crowded into the school gymnasium to watch the final show. They screamed every time Kelly appeared on the gymnasium's three big screens.

Kelly sings for her fans after they voted her the American Idol.

The winner was announced just seven minutes before the two-hour episode ended. Kelly had won 58 percent of the nationwide call-in vote. She was the new American Idol. "I didn't actually hear them say I won," she told reporters later. "Justin just hugged me."

Success!

Overnight, Kelly had become a superstar. She now had a **recording contract** with RCA for $1 million. She immediately began a whirlwind **media** tour. She appeared on *The Tonight Show with Jay Leno*, the *Today* show, and *LIVE with Regis and Kelly*.

After a brief beach vacation, Kelly went to work. She sang the national anthem at the Lincoln Memorial on September 11, 2002. She gave interviews, filmed a video, and prepared for her first record release.

Kelly's first **single** arrived in stores on September 17. The single included the songs "A Moment Like This" and "Before Your Love." The single **debuted** at number 60 on *Billboard* magazine's Hot 100. It quickly climbed to number 52. Then, in one week, it shot from number 52 to number one!

Kelly Clarkson on The Tonight Show with Jay Leno

Idol to Idol

On September 23, Kelly was featured in the television special "American **Idol** in Vegas." The special reunited Kelly with all 30 of her original *American Idol* costars. It also gave her the chance to sing a **duet** with her own idol, Reba McEntire.

Two weeks later, Kelly and the other *American Idol* finalists hit the road for a concert tour. The group performed nearly 30 shows around the nation. Fans unable to attend the concert could buy the *American Idol Greatest Moments* CD. The CD was released October 1.

Kelly's next challenge is in the recording studio. A full album of her songs will be released in early 2003. **Professional** songwriters will compose most of the songs. However, Kelly is hoping to get some of her own material on the album. It's one of several goals for the energetic young Texan who has become the American Idol.

Kelly sings with her idol, Reba McEntire, during "American Idol in Vegas."

Glossary

a cappella - without musical accompaniment.

audience - a group of people watching a performance.

audition - a short performance to test a performer's ability.

contractor - someone who agrees to do work or supply materials.

critique - to review a performance.

debut - a first appearance.

demo - a recording made to demonstrate the talent of a singer.

duet - a song sung by two performers.

episode - one show in a continuing series of shows.

idol - a figure that others look up to and respect.

karaoke - a machine that provides background music for a singer.

lozenge - a small piece of candy containing sugar or medicine.

media - communication companies, such as the news media.

professional - working for money rather than for pleasure.

recording contract - an agreement between a performer and a record company to produce an album.

recruit - to get someone to join a group.

single - one song from an album, sold by itself.

sophisticated - mature and controlled.

vocal - related to the voice.

wardrobe - a collection of clothing.

Web Sites

Would you like to learn more about Kelly Clarkson? Please visit **www.abdopub.com** to find up-to-date Web site links about the American Idol. These links are routinely monitored and updated to provide the most current information available.

Index

J
B   Wheeler, Jill C.,
Clarkson   1964-
W   Kelly Clarkson.